For Noé, Malo,
Jules, and Lucie

M.R.

IMPRIMATUR
+ Most Reverend Robert J. McManus, S.T.D.
Bishop of Worcester
December 24, 2019

Pflaum Publishing Group
3055 Kettering Blvd., Suite 100
Dayton, OH 45439
800-543-4383
Pflaum.com

ISBN: 978-1-94735-824-9
Printed in China.

bayard A division of Bayard, Inc.

Text by Élodie Maurot • Illustrations by Maud Riemann

The Sacrament of Baptism

BECOMING PART OF GOD'S FAMILY

Pflaum
SACRAMENTAL PREPARATION

“Baptism is mysterious to me. What happens?”

Anne, 9 years old

“Who can be baptized?”

Tom, 7 years old

"How does Baptism make me closer to Jesus?"

Olga, 10 years old

"Why is Baptism so important?"

Lucas, 11 years old

Have you heard about Baptism? Do you wonder what it is?

This book will help answer your questions.

What is Baptism?

Baptism is the sacrament that helps you become a Christian and enter into the family of Christians, called the **Church**.

For **Catholics**, Baptism is like a second birth. The water of Baptism is a sign of dying with Christ and then rising again with him into new life. It marks the start of a new life with God. All Christians, must be baptized.

*Words in **bold** are key words and are defined on pages 60–61.*

What is a sacrament?

A sacrament is a sign of grace that allows Catholics to see and welcome the saving love of God. During the celebration of a sacrament, specific actions are performed and special words are spoken. Baptism is the first sacrament we receive.

Discovering Jesus Christ

Jesus was a man who lived in Galilee two thousand years ago. For Christians then and today, this man is the Son of God. Why do they believe that? It's a long story....

Jesus, the friend of God

Jesus was from Galilee. He was **Jewish** and lived in Nazareth with people who were waiting for the coming of the Messiah, the messenger of God.

As people listened to him and watched how he lived, they realized that this man was not like other men.

Jesus spoke of God as a friend, as a father, as his Father. He announced that the **Kingdom of God** is near.

He paid attention to little children, the weak, the sick.
He gave courage to those who were hopeless.
He welcomed those who were rejected.

He shared the love of God with everyone around him!

Jesus made friends

Men and women decided to follow Jesus: they did not really know who this man was, but they felt happy being with him. They became his companions, his **disciples**. Jesus told them about God and life. When they listened to him, they were amazed. They saw in Jesus

the sign that God is close to us. Some began to believe that this man was the messenger of God, the Messiah.

How do we know the story of Jesus?

The early Christians told about the life of Jesus in four books called the ***Gospels****. Non-Christian historians of the time also spoke about Jesus in their books. We are sure that Jesus really existed.*

Jesus, True God and True Man

Jesus is the Son of God. He is the Second Person of the Holy Trinity—God the Father, God the Son, and God the Holy Spirit. Jesus said that God loves us all and wants us to love others in the same way. He said that God wants us to have a good heart and be kind to those around us.

Jesus wasn't afraid to get close to those who were rejected. He spoke of God being friends with all people.

The religious leaders of his time were angry. Who was this man who believed he was above religious rules? The Romans, who ruled the country, were afraid of scandal and riots. The enemies of Jesus plotted together to put him to death.

Jesus was tortured and killed

Jesus' enemies arrested him. After a quick trial, he was tortured and nailed to a cross like a criminal.

Before he died, Jesus said, "There is no greater love than to give your life for your friends."

Jesus was willing to die for us because he wanted us to be able to go to Heaven to be with God. He wanted us to know that God loves us freely and is willing to forgive our sins.

He is alive!

But for the friends of Jesus,
the story did not stop there.
Jesus came to see them and let
them know that he was alive. He
had been raised from the dead!
God's love overcame death
and conquered it.

Jesus is risen, and now he is
alive forever. Surely this man
is the Son of God!

Eternal life with Jesus

It is very difficult for us to imagine what ***eternal life*** *is like. What we know is what Jesus told us: that eternal life is a life that lasts forever. It is a life of love enjoyed with God and other people in Heaven. There is no sickness or pain or sorrow in eternal life with Jesus.*

The first Christian Baptisms

After Jesus' **Resurrection**, his friends told others about his life, Death, and Resurrection.

They welcomed all who believed that Jesus died and rose again. They baptized with water "in the name of the Father, the Son, and the Holy Spirit." In other words, they baptized in the name of God: the Father who is the **Creator**; Jesus, who is both truly God and truly human; and the Holy Spirit, who is the breath of God's love.

A very old sign

In ancient religions, water was used as a sign of purification. Some ***Jewish people*** *of Jesus' day also used water to show that they were turning to God. Jesus was baptized by John the Baptist. For Christians, Baptism has a new meaning: it is the beginning of a new, eternal life with God.*

Baptism through the centuries

Beginning with the first Christians and continuing to the present time, the Church welcomes new Christians though the Sacrament of Baptism.

Baptism at the time of the Romans

A Baptism in the Middle Ages

A Baptism in colonial times

A Baptism today.

Who is baptized?

At the beginning of Christianity, adults were baptized. Soon, it became usual to baptize children too. Today, the Church baptizes both children and adults. Parents should have their babies baptized soon after they are born.

Preparing for Baptism

A young person or adult who wants to be baptized has to learn what the **Catholic Church** teaches. It is a journey that brings a person closer to God.

On the way!

When a young person or adult wants to be baptized, they go to a Catholic church and join the preparation program. Those who are interested in being baptized prepare together as a group. The preparation usually lasts one year and consists of several steps. At each step, a person chooses to continue or decides to stop the preparation. When a baby is baptized, his or her parents must go through a shorter preparation program at the church.

Rite of Christian Initiation for Adults, Adapted for Children (RCIA)

In the RCIA adapted for children, children age 7 and up who were not baptized as infants or who have not received any formal teaching, learn about the ***faith****. They attend religious formation classes and are included in the RCIA rituals during Mass and other celebrations.*

ADULT BAPTISM

First Step: The Rite of Acceptance into the order of catechumens

This ceremony is the first step on the path to Baptism.
The community of Christians welcomes those who are interested in joining the Church, who are now called catechumens. The **priest** calls each person by name and presents them to the community. When someone decides to prepare for Baptism, it's a very happy occasion.

Second Step: Rite of Election of enrollment of names

During this step, those who wish to be baptized begin to learn more about Jesus Christ and the teachings of Church found in the *Catechism of the Catholic Church.*

Catechumens receive the Sign of the Cross, the sign that Christians use to recall the life, Death and Resurrection of Jesus.

The catechumens are introduced to the Gospels, which tell the story of Jesus' life and how his friends gradually discovered that he was the Son of God. The Gospels are part of the **Bible**.

They also learn about the teachings and traditions of the Catholic Church.

Third Step: Celebration of the Sacraments of Initiation

At the time of Baptism, young people and adults entering the Church will also receive two other sacraments: Confirmation and the Eucharist. These sacraments, along with Baptism, are called the Sacraments of Christian Initiation. But the first sacrament is Baptism!

The day of Baptism

This is it! The big day has finally arrived …
the day of Baptism.

Welcome to the Church!

Baptism is always a time of celebration. Family, friends, godparents, and the whole Church family gather to welcome new members. Baptisms often take place on Sundays because that is the day of the week when we recall the Resurrection of Jesus—his rising from death to life. Baptisms also might happen at the Easter Vigil since that is when Catholics gather to celebrate the Resurrection in a special way.

Godparents or sponsors

Godparents or sponsors agree to help a person being baptized to know Jesus Christ. Infants and children must have at least one Catholic godparent. They are like a big brother and a big sister with whom a young person can talk about God. Adults usually choose Catholic friends as their sponsors.

God reminds us of his love

God has always loved each of us with a special love. On the day of our Baptism, God reminds us of that love. God tells those who are baptized that they are important, that they have value, and that they are loved with an everlasting love.

On the day of our Baptism, we respond to God's love and choose to make a **covenant** with him. At that point, we become sons or daughters of God. The saving power of Jesus and the **sanctifying grace** of the Holy Spirit wash away **Original Sin**. Baptism is the first sacrament for the **forgiveness of sins**.

The Word of God

The Bible is the Word of God. It is the record of what God has done throughout history and in people's hearts. The Bible tells us that God, who is our Father, is close to us. He loves us and wants to make a covenant with us.

Saying "no" to evil

The priest asks if the person being baptized is ready to reject evil and sin. Sin is everything that hurts and stops love and prevents a person from being loving.

If the person being baptized agrees to reject evil, they answer, "I do."

The faith of Christians

The priest asks if the person believes in God the Father; in God's only Son, Jesus Christ, who died and rose from the dead; and in the Holy Spirit, the strength of love and the life of God.

He then asks if the person believes in the Catholic Church, in the **Communion of Saints**, in the in the **forgiveness of sins**, in the **resurrection of the body**, and in eternal life.

The person shows their acceptance of the Catholic faith by answering "I do" to each of the questions.

The water of Baptism

Water is the sign of life. Without water, no life could exist on earth: no plants, animals, or people.

The water of Baptism symbolizes our dying with Christ and then rising again with him into new life.

What is a symbol?

A symbol is like poetry. It's a way of making things understandable in an imaginative way. To explain what happens at the time of Baptism, Christians use three symbols: water, oil, and light.

"I baptize you ..."

The priest or deacon pours water on the head of the person being baptized three times, saying, "I baptize you in the name of the Father, the Son, and the Holy Spirit." Sometimes the baptized person is dipped three times into a pool of water. This is called Baptism by immersion. On the day of Baptism, the person is immersed in water and in the new life of Jesus.

The baptized person is now ready for a new life with God.

The word *baptism*

Baptism *comes from a Greek word that means "immersion." The person being baptized is immersed in water and rises out of the water, filled with the new life of Jesus.*

Holy Oil

The priest makes a Sign of the Cross with consecrated oil on the forehead of the person being baptized. This holy oil is called the Sacred Chrism.

It is a sign of the Holy Spirit, the Spirit of life and the love of God. The Sacred Chrism indicates that the baptized person belongs to Christ.

Its sweet smell is a reminder that it is sweet and pleasant to be a friend of God.

Where does the word *Christ* come from?

This word comes from the Greek Christos, *meaning "anointed." Jesus is "the Christ" because he has a unique mission to save the world.*

Candle and white clothing

The person being baptized often receives a candle lit from another candle called the Paschal candle. The Paschal candle represents the Risen Christ, the Light of the World. The person may also receive a white garment.

The candle represents the light of Christ. The white garment represents the new life of grace we receive in Baptism. The baptized person now shines that light into the world. It is a light that is stronger than sadness and death.

One Baptism for all Christians

For all Christians, Baptism is very important.

There is only one Baptism for all Christians: Catholics, **Protestants**, and **Orthodox Christians**. All Christians recognize each other as brothers and sisters. Baptism is celebrated only once in life.

Orthodox children are often baptized as infants. They are baptized by immersion which means they are immersed entirely in water.

What happens after Baptism?

Baptism is not the end of the road...it is the beginning! With the Good News of the Word of God and the help of other Christians, those who are baptized are able to respond to the love of God in a new way. God wants all of us to have abundant life and happiness. God wants everyone to feel deeply alive and happy.

In the Bible, Saint Paul wrote: “For freedom Christ has set us free” (Galatians 5:1). Our freedom is precious in the eyes of God.

God gives you strength

After receiving Baptism, a young person or an adult will make their First Communion. Then, at the same Mass, they eat the bread and drink the wine that are the true Body and Blood of Jesus Christ, the real presence of God. This sacrament is given to Christians so that they can grow closer to God and to others.

By praying, reading the Word of God, and being attentive to our words and deeds, we will always discover more about who God is and how much he loves us.

We are friends of God, and God asks us to be friends of justice and defenders of the poor. Get ready to commit to a new life!

Painting, dance, scientific research...everything that makes the world more beautiful and more humane pleases God.

God wants to be known. Christians are invited make the love of God visible in their own unique ways.

Questions about Baptism

What if someone has questions about God? Can they be baptized?

We can never know everything about God, but we can choose to trust him. Faith doesn't exist without risk or moments of uncertainty, but we can count on God, who already loves us even with our doubts.

Can anyone be baptized?

Yes. Whether a person is rich or poor, young or old, lives in Africa or America, anyone can be baptized.

Is Baptism magic?

Not at all. God doesn't decide for us or take away our free will. We are not God's puppets. God wants us to be free, because only those who are free can truly love.

Does God love those who aren't baptized?

Of course! God's love does not stop at the borders of our families or our churches. God does not look at who is baptized before loving them. God's love is infinite, and it reaches everyone. But in Baptism, we answer "yes" to the love of God. This gives God great joy!

Key Words

Bible. The book that tells the story of God's interaction with humanity.

Catholic. This word means "universal" in Greek. The **catholic church** (lowercased) is the family of all Christian believers. But the **Catholic Church** (capitalized) recognizes the Pope as its head, the bishops as successors of Jesus' Apostles, and all believers with them as members of the Body of Christ.

Church. The family of Christians. The same word in lowercase also denotes the building where Christians gather to pray and worship.

Communion of Saints. The family of God's friends of yesterday and today. To believe in the Communion of Saints is to believe that the friends of God are still alive in Heaven, thanks to Jesus' Death on the Cross.

covenant. To make a covenant is to make a special agreement with someone, to be united in a special relationship with them.

Creator. God created the sky, the earth, and everything that lives in it. The Bible tells us that men and women are specially created "in God's image."

disciples. Friends of Jesus; those who follow him.

eternal life. The mysterious life after death; endless life, with God, in love.

faith. To have faith in God is to believe and trust in God in a special way.

forgiveness of sins. Sin is what separates us from God and other people. This stops love and prevents love. To ask for forgiveness for sin is to ask God to pardon us for the wrong we have done.

Gospel. The Good News of God's love announced by Jesus Christ. The Gospels are books that tell about this Good News. They are part of the Bible.

Jewish people. These are the people of the Bible with whom God has made a covenant. The religion of the Jewish people is Judaism. Jesus, his family, and his friends were Jewish.

Kingdom of God. The special phrase Jesus used to describe the kind of life that God wants for us, a world full of justice and love.

Original Sin. The sin of the first human beings and the loss of grace their sin caused.

Orthodox Christians. Christians who have been separated from the Catholic Church since the eleventh century. They share many of the same beliefs as Catholics.

Priest. An ordained man who serves a community of Catholics. His role includes celebrating Mass and the sacraments, as well as explaining the Bible and living a good Christian life as an example to others.

Protestants. Christians who have been separated from the Catholic Church since the sixteenth century. They share some of the same beliefs as Catholics.

resurrection of the body. To believe that our body and soul are not finally destroyed by death but one day will be reunited with God forever in Heaven.

Resurrection. The passage of Jesus from death to life on the third day after his Crucifixion. The Resurrection is a central truth of our faith.

sanctifying grace. The grace that heals our sinful human nature by giving us a share in the divine life of the Trinity. Sanctifying grace was earned for us by the suffering and Death of Jesus Christ. It enables us to live as God's children.

Also Available

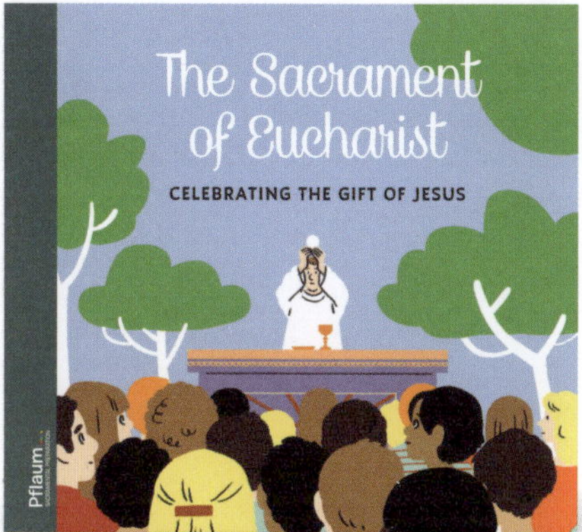

PRODUCT CODE: HTP-6303 ISBN: 978-1-94735-826-3

PRODUCT CODE: HTP-6302 ISBN: 978-1-94735-825-6

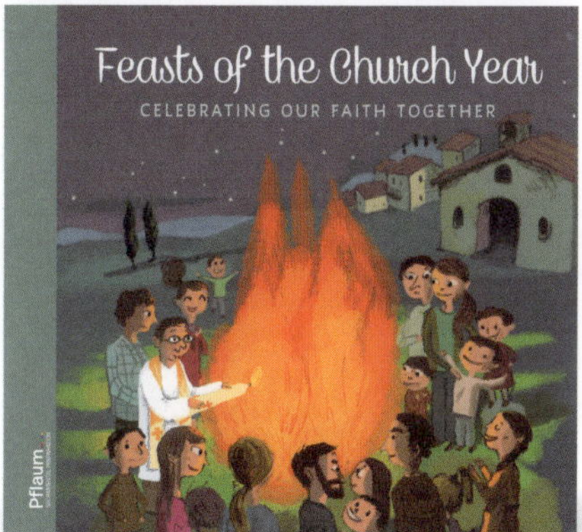

PRODUCT CODE: HTP-6304 ISBN: 978-1-94735-827-0

This new set of children's books has been adapted for use with older children preparing for the First Sacraments as well as RCIA, Adapted for Children. Each book's content offers an overview of a sacrament while the Liturgical Year title helps children learn about the Church's feasts and seasons.

TO ORDER: pflaum.com
1-800-543-4383

Pflaum
SACRAMENTAL PREPARATION